All the While
The Tides of Humber Flow

W. R. Burnett

ELEVENTH HOUR PRESS

All the While
The Tides of Humber
Flow

W. R. Burnett

Eleventh Hour Press Limited
P.O. Box 14640
Welsh Harp Village
London NW9 7WL
e-mail eleventhhourpress@yahoo.com
Registered in England
Company No. 3389610

First published 2000
Eleventh Hour Press Limited

ISBN   1-902025-03-2

A CIP catalogue record for this book is available from the British
Library.

Typeset in Perpetua

Printed and bound by
The Old Hall Press
Old Hall Green, Ware
Hertfordshire, SG11 1DU

*Dedicated to my dear wife Dora who died in February 1998,
and to my daughters Margaret and Hilary.*

*Grateful thanks to Teresa Gallagher, Jim Mulligan and
Hilary Lennon for their hard work on my behalf.*

Summer Refugee

Buzzing, droning, sad Bluebottle,
These are November's doleful days;
Yet you fly around our house full of bother
Searching for summer's golden rays.

Summer has gone, swept far away,
High o'er the wolds, swift out to sea,
And though you drone in the house all day
Never will summer return for thee.

Non-stop rasps as an elfin saw-mill
Reverberates on our window pane,
As drumming above the window-sill
You strive to escape, but all in vain.

In August's azure, drowsy days,
On sunshine airs by hedges and trees,
Contented flew among verdant ways,
Bluebottles, butterflies, wasps and bees.

Now are all fled, vanished away,
Swift o'er the wolds, high o'er the sea,
September's chills warned them not to delay,
All have departed – all except thee,

So you are the last; one all alone,
Desolate, desperate, frenzied and sad.
And echo of summer, left to bemoan,
In autumn limbo until you go mad.

Please, seek a small hole wherein you may dream
The harsh winter through, secure from all hurt;
And when in your cave spring thrusts lancing beams,
Come forth, dear bluebottles, and buzz till you burst.

Per Ardua Ad Astra

Three long hard years are past and gone,
The treasured prize doubt's depressing,
By weary toil success achieved,
A mind from anxious thought relieved.

From marshy flats of daily care,
Cloyed down with doubts depressing fare,
A path was climbed by hardships ways
To upland heights and sunlit days.

A teacher, signed and sealed am I,
Examined, tested, screened, I cry,
By Thomas Huxley College sent,
Approved and passed by Government.

How fortunate is England's realm,
With my firm hand on teaching's helm
My little angels, pupils raw,
Upon my features gaze with awe.

How kind to them has fortune been,
By choosing such a mentor keen,
Each one by me well taught and bright,
How can they fail in life's stern fight?

Through evening's tranquil hour I rest,
Refreshment for tomorrow's zest,
In class I shall their future speed
To sure success and splendid deed.

Ithaca

Well, here am I, an old worn man,
As sailor cast upon an unknown shore,
And on this strand forever must abide
Till cold-faced death doth lead me,
As a Friend, towards his door

Yet firstly might I only walk by Humber's tide,
Surged forth by Holland's vast grey seas,
And attentive to the gulls harsh cries,
Perchance may glimpse a ghostly Viking Fleet.

But naught care I, my time is near,
And neither Norse nor Dane afright.
Let them sail on, in day's pale light,
Till all are drowned by darkened night.

Let me but lie my head by Riding's shores,
And breathe the air 'neath Yorkshire's skies,
Then will I surely die content,
To rest at peace for evermore.

Hilda and I

This is a tale of a lady called Hilda
Whose husband fondly determined to build her
A nice little cottage, alongside the ocean,
A fine sand beach, a pleasant location
Wherein they could dwell, no strife of employment,
Through years of retirement, in tranquil enjoyment,

But Hilda, sweet Hilda, come steal off with me,
Abjure you, I beg you, a life by the Sea
Let us speed off together – just you and I
Away from the ocean to the mountains we'll fly
Where Hilda, dear Hilda, we'll wander alone
Among the high crags and start a new home.

Then Hilda, fair Hilda, in noondays clear light
Or moon's silvered rays we'll look down from our height
To the far distant shore, to a man and a house,
To a tiny squat dwelling, to a man like a mouse
A tiny wan figure who shuffles and sighs

Among the sand dunes, amidst the gull's cries,
But Hilda, my Hilda, he must manage alone
Down there, by himself, beside the sea's foam,
While we dwell in the clouds, absorbed in each other
And for him, the poor creature, we just cannot bother,

My darling, my dear one, up here in the heather
Time floats like a bird on zephyrs of pleasure.

By the hard pebbled beach, the wind's stinging spray,
A grey sullen sea at sinking of day,
He wanders along by the sad lonely shore
Just a speck on the strand next the wave's hollow roar
But up here we're close heaven, as happy can be,
And we care not a fig for the man by the sea.

A Cry for Assurance

This shining sea of limpid prose,
Of jewelled word and silvered phase,
Is as a bright-dewed morning rose,
For your enchantment here arrayed.

Yet as I scan my lines again,
Disturbing doubts come stealing in.
O say not all is labour vain
And voices praising ne'er shall ring.
O can these verses only be
Mere forays in futility.

Evening Bells

A plaintive peal of village bells
Falls thin and clear on evening airs,
In fading light carillons tell –
Of long past years, of times despairs.

And lives, deep gone, left dim behind
Are slowly stirred by each high toll,
Grey vap'rous mists rise, undefined,
Each wisp a wraith, a forlorn soul.

Each shadow raised by calling bells
Does palely wait as abstract moon
Pallid shines – through opaque night
Upon their weathered, obscure tombs.

The long dark fades; no trumpets sound
With flowing dawn; no blaze in distant sky,
The trembling mists steal to the ground
As dreams, and leave, behind a whispered sigh.

The earth enfolds night's mysteries
From countless prying eyes of day,
And serried gravestones guardians stand
Above each narrow bed of clay.

Heaven's far tides surge in unknown places,
Creation's face is hidden from sight,
Hope is a silver thread to salvation
For naught else remains but unending night.

Then peel no more you sweet-toned bells;
Coldly sleeping let them lay
In silence next their blanching bones
Awaiting Heaven's judgment day.

The Old Man

O'er a rough gravelled path half hidden by bushes
Sun's clear morning rays night's mists are dispersing,
Here I see jewelled webs linking dew-heavy rushes
And hear, from afar, dawn birds call rehearsing.
But my thoughts drift in despond, in undefined sorrow,
I wear out each day for another to follow.

This abandoned old lane seems to mirror my life,
The path these feet tread a grey pattern of living.
Would I welcome its close on yon blue-shaded skyline,
At barrier of briars at farthest sights edge
Marking the place where the rutted way closes,
Setting the hour when life's journey shall end.

In time long ago was this path a swift highway,
Busy with movement at noon's thronged array
Time past was this man in his eager bright years
Youthful and strong, a stranger to fears
But harsh winters have wasted, worn both to decay,
Gentle sunshine restored not in summer's soft stay.

High above anchored fields another world circles,
A crystalline domain, soundless, serene,
Floating free on blue oceans of heaven's wide spaces
Sail cloud-silver islands and far mountain ranges.

Does the Lord of Creation, from deep fathoms of silence
Coldly regard, with transcendental wisdom,
Observant, percipient, detached and uncaring,
My guilts and my follies, lost hopes and sad yearnings.

Beware Dark Night

In rural spread of curtained nests
We humans two find obscure rest,
As low-roofed tortoises we dwell,
Our bungalow a tortoise shell;
Locked secure each threatened night
When shadows clutch the threat of light.
Safe though the world with darkness fills,
And hidden witches cast their spells.

Then grasshoppers, grown giant size,
Regard our home with hooded eyes;
They stalk about on heron's legs
And high bestride the garden hedge;
Leave curious footprints as they pass,
Implanted on the dewy grass,
Beneath the stars they squeaky cry
To hushed tall trees where mute owls hide.

These upstart monsters weirdly prance
The midnight hour in grotesque dance
Until the queenly moon dissuades
Such fevered sport and mad displays
Long night shades grey, the warned moon flies
Afar to rule the orient skies;
Where Ceylon's temple bells are stirred
And spices perfume Java's hills.

Now grasshoppers themselves take heed
And shrink to minute size with speed
In flood of fear for coming dawn
When all things normal patterns form,
When mystic, creeping, half-seen shapes
Dissolve away in vap'rous haste,
Bereft dark shield night sinks and dies
Day gives back sight to sightless eyes.
So, as the turmoiled night is o'er
Two human heads around the door
Peer timid forth; four wary eyes
The soothing calm of morn espy;
A thousand shafts of light are cast
As diamonds on the dewy grass,
Where grasshoppers hide quite unseen,
Tiny, fragile, unesteemed.

Slow hibernation hours have passed,
Safe are we humans, brave, relaxed.
Our easy hearts, the busy day,
Dispel all foolishness away.
The lawn to cut without a care
Of insect life-forms lurking there.
We are the earth's inheritors;
That is, until night comes once more.

Ode to a Reluctant House Painter

Oh Swetez, dear Swetez, please send me thy bill,
For my fears o'er its size grow apace,
And thought's tangled skein doth weave a sharp chill,
While a debtor's prison induces disgrace.

The postman calls not at morning's clear light,
Though the lark sings sweet on the hill,
And the sun's fairest rays shed no delight,
Though they golden frame our dear daffodils.

Hoarded coins do I count when day is done,
I arrange them in neat ordered rows,
As soldiers to face your bill's heavy sum;
Yet shadows deepen as darkness grows.

So I pray thee, dear Swetez, bestir thyself,
And instant despatch my account this day,
Then solace may come, despite vanished wealth,
And barefoot and buoyant I'll stroll life's ways.

Dawn

The sparkling eye, the ready smile
Of kindly heart, bereft of guile,
A blend of harmony and grace,
In bloom of youth on Dawn's fair face.

Here brains and beauty are arrayed,
Six medals 'O', hard won, displayed.
Good fortune aid ability,
To grant her true felicity.

A Moon Miscellany

From out the cold sea, dripping wet
A darken'd sea, whence sun has set,
Comes glistening Moon in bright array
Sprinkling drops of saline spray
Upon the foam of sandy shores
Where none has ever trod before
A lustrous wave-line radiance
From silver sphere's beneficence.
Now doth the Moon rise heavenward
To view the Holderness wide sward,
And adds its drips to night-time dews
To sprinkle cows, lambs, foals and ewes,
To seaweed drop as token charms
And dampen hayricks, farms and barns.
Perchance a few bewilder'd fish
May hapless grace some breakfast dish,
And pale endure blind Fortune's wheel
To fates the ocean's stars conceal

The reigning Queen, herself fresh bathed,
(as Venus from the blue deeps raised)
Floats high above the land below
And graciously her glow bestows....
Beneath, the sleeping hamlets lie,
And, on the far horizon's sky

May faint be seen a distant bulk,
A seeming shipwreck'd foundered hulk,
Which is a seaport, Kingston's Town,
Enrolled in history's renown;
Where life is real, and earnest too,
And all folk there are brave and true,
And even if they sombre seem
'Tis that they seldom pause to dream,
But dig and delve and constant spin
To guard against each winter's chill

Earth's firmament, in Moon's descent,
And Time itself, both sigh consent.
She sinks where Riding's Pennine's rise,
Where hill-side heather shyly hides.
Her silver wings she fold in rest,
And all is silence, all is blest.

New morning scene comes fair and bright,
The Humber tide repulses night,
And this poor scribe, at Hull's Old Town,
Doth turn towards his humble round.
Leaves pier and cobbled lanes behind,
Which ancient are and close confined.
Here sandall'd friars early stepped
Where these two feet now careful fret.
(For, wingless, never should one try
Upon the daylight air to fly).

To gate-less Whitefriargate I go
By improved pavements, heel and toe,
These trailing gowns and hooded faces
Are vap'rous friars meditative;
And, if unseen by instant shoppers,
Are visible each to the others....
Lurks here John Hotham next the moat?
Pray – fall ye not in, King Charles's ghost,
But this the stuff of moonlight themes
Strange fevered thoughts from shadow'd dreams.
Such wild miscellany of mind
Should surely move to present times.

Just further on, Victoria Square,
Where traffic, noise and people are,
And in the centre, boldly placed,
Hull's finest toilets, marble graced.
A circled mound one notes at first,
And hid below, the working parts.

High on the mound, herself alone,
Is Good Queen Vic upon her throne
With haughty eye does she look down
Upon her subjects all around
In royal gaze, quite sublimal
Mistress of a large urinal.

(19)

Now chimes Guildhall the noon-day hour
And I still far from my home bower.
With new resolve I'll haste along
To catch the bus to Cottingham.
Reality! I'll grasp thy hand
And tread on solids, not on sand.
So dreams and common-sense shall be
An intermingled harmony....

O come again thou silver Queen,
Illume our plain with thy pure beams.
The velvet skies thy gardens are
The flowers there but tended stars.
Mistress ephemeral of the night!
O glowing sphere of wondrous light.
O'er wooded vale and grassy lea
'Forever charm the world and me.

Humber Bridge

The pleasant pictures here displayed
Portray some Yorkshire parts of grace,
How sad the lot of those who breathe
Less fresher airs in southern fields.

The Humber may be likened to
The tumbling torrents of Peru,
But eye's delight is blighted by
An iron bridge thrust in the sky.

And York and Lincoln's stretching shores
Are now enchained for evermore,
In durance vile lie languishing
'Till Earth's last trumpet call shall ring.

Fled far away the builders bold,
Here bridgemen garner meager tolls,
For sparse the motorists as they pass
Across a wide and watery gap.

With Charon and the river Styx
Comparisons perchance persist;
Yet let sweet Homer rest in peace,
Bereft of views from Hessle's beach.

At noon's first light the bridge stands clear,
As lord of all beyond compare,
But misted moons at night do see
A monstrous spider fantasy.

Silver'd gulls from wheaten fields,
About the towers dive and wheel
Yet sad below the waters ride
Voyaging to Holland's tides.

Hull Thoughts

By Hull's Green Ginger's narrow lane
Cling memories of ancient fame.
Tall-masted ships no longer bring
Orient spices from Qingping.

High Skidby's windmill, turning there,
To Cottingham wafts pleasant airs,
And where the beck so softly flows
Are cockatoos and flamingoes.

We old ones in our crescent caves
Do New Year wishes here convey.
We hope and trust the long months through
True happiness will bring to you.

Mixed Seasonal Thoughts

All festive cheer,
Mince pies, plum duffs,
And also nuts,
Are linked with Christmas as a must.
Together they emit
An aura on the air
Which humans may absorb
All free from fear.
The inert turkey can no message send,
His destiny he has fulfilled,
And met his end.

In creeps the New Year
With tears as rain,
The carcass of the turkey is
Thrown in the bin,
Just bones and skin,
Upon the council refuse dump it lies
And ghostly dreams.
The pies, the duffs,
As well as nuts,
Are also gone,
What was their final end?
But, in this matter
Perhaps 'tis better
Not to dwell upon.

A November Ode

Season of fogs and funeral corteges,
Of early dusks and reluctant dawns,
Of weeping willows and aimless purposes
Pale echoes of joy by despairs foresworn.

Forebodings of Christmas tinseled happiness,
Brave new year vows born to be broke,
Of roses decayed and noon days greyness,
Each falling leaf a fallen hope.

Expand, I beg thee, oh ozone opening,
Bring brightness and warmth to our sad, dreary ways,
Uplift we downcast homo sapiens,
Cut the bonds of the wheel of these dismal days.

Then may heaven's blue a dreaming ocean paint,
On a shining sea-shore may we find our peace.
Untroubled, unhurried, felicitous persons
In golden sunlight in precious release.

The Calendar

Twelve printed months hung on the wall,
A captured year in numbered thrall,
Such strictly columned figures are
Inscrutable beyond compare.
Perchance if they should move around
Each enclosed sheet without a sound
'Twould make then much more friendly seem
Much closer to the daily need,
But such unlikely stirrings are
Vague wisps of thought upon the air.
Yet if you gaze with inward mind
May you a hidden mirror find
With landscape wide, a gentle breeze,
And cockatoos in baob trees.
But hush, I pray you silence keep
Within this land aroused from sleep.
Step softly on the pebbl'd shore
That curves, white-foamed, for evermore,
Where a mermaid from a shining sea
Sits and sings her songs to thee
Of lands forlorn, of coral isles,
Of dragon moons at midnight skies.
Pale nymph beside a silver sea,
Who sings her mystic songs to thee –
And then is gone; the mirrored shore,
The land, the sky, is seen no more

But fades away as dreams released
To dream no more in timeless sleep;
In farthest caverns, there to lie,
'til strange new suns enlarge the sky....
This calendar, first day begun,
Signposts ahead all weeks to come.
A birth in ice, in snow the grave,
As season's pendulum doth sway
In order due, 'twixt chill and heat,
High summer's gold or winter's sleet,
May Fortune kind attend your days,
And sweetly steal the hours away

Random Thoughts at Christmas

Bleak the winds o'er Yorkshire's tundra's,
Where fearful hides the fleeing year
Yet southward are Arcadian pastures
And fairest Neath lies dreaming there.
Ah, thou Wales of song and legend,
Woods, vales and limpid streams,
Silver'd fish the waters leaping,
Leap to flash in sunlit gleams.

In Wales abounds the joys of Christmas,
Festivities in house and home,
The roasted turkey's inert promise,
While gas-fire yule logs bravely glow.

Balding, self-important husbands,
Plump and perm'd and busy wives
Go about the season's pleasures,
Gemutlichkeit for middle lives.
Innocent the lads and lassies
Gambol at their party joys,
Curtained corners, pulsing passes,
All the frolics youth employs
Mistletoe, impromptu dances
Noise and laughter loud rebound,
Stereos and soulful glances,
Flushed are faces all around.

In the daytime's healthy breezes,
On the wet and muddied fields,
Come the rugby players pounding,
Studded boots and iron knees.
Down the line as arrow flighting
Speeds a wingman, ball safe clutching,
But in the heaving maelstrom mauls
What need be there for any ball?

Snowbound are the northern crescent caves,
Fainter yet the human footprints lie,
Fierce and long do blow the winter gales,
More desolate the land, more grey the leaden sky,
Far off in Wales of song and legend,
Fair folk tread out green pastured ways;
The shelter'd bays reflect the curve of heaven,
And Merlin walks in moonlight's pale array

Summer Nightmare

The long night watches of gardener's woes
Are haunted by shadowy greenfly foes,
Yet flee they not when morning light glows,
But harden to life to attack the sweet rose.

Airborne pests with no natural foes
Excepting I with my derris dust blows,
Who daily doth strive to guard the fair rose
From the small green flies with the long green nose,

On the bushes bloom the damask rose,
Guarded by me from these slant-eyed foes;
For one purpose in life I'm here I suppose
A guardian knight for a damask rose.

All desperate summer the hard struggle goes
'Gainst the small green flies with the long green nose;
And none understand for none can know
How weary with strife my spirit grows.

And when in winter the winter snows
White carpet the land so nothing grows,
Then, only then, may I take repose,
And sombre reflect the snows will go.

In fevered fancies the greenflies grow,
Monstrous, malignant, beneath the snow,
Until, in spring, great millions flow
And swarm the world to overthrow.

Lengthened fang and basilisk eye,
Green gleaning clouds across the sky,
By squadron's flight to tile and dive
And seize earth's rich fields that dreaming lie.

'N'eath summer's sun the roses will grow,
And greenfly also, as well I know
Please stay frosty days, please stay white snow,
And let for ever the winter winds blow.

November

November is a limping old sun,
Of misted fields and bare balding trees,
Dark shelter he seeks as soon as he can,
To lie in woods as a beggar concealed.

Funeral queues he attends in grey churchyards,
Where coffins are lowered in solemn way,
Where the vicar lifts eyes, to high heavenwards,
But the coffins stay low in the yellow clay.

Church bells slow toll along the lane,
And re-echo around for the coffin'd dead,
All the mourners return the way they came,
On a carpet of leaves live footsteps tread.

And the vicar goes home to muffins for tea,
And tiny bulb tips catch the last of the sun,
But the recent dead have nothing to see,
For the sun and the bulbs forever are gone.

And the limping old man goes back to the trees,
To lie in a wood as a beggar concealed,
And colder he gets as his month drifts on,
For December will finish him off you see.

British Summertime

In city and in village
At farmsteads and in flat
Our clocks have we put forward
Turned forward, never back
The stars in their bright courses
Do dutiful comply
That stern decree from London
Twere wise not to defy,
From shepherd in the gloaming,
Of clerk at early morn,
No querulous complaining
By any shall be borne.

Large clocks fixed high at stations,
Small mantelpiece stood clocks,
In careful correlation
Go they tick-tock-tick-tock.
All menfolk and women
All husbands and their wives,
School children, demure children,
To new hours set their lives.
The nation thus goes forward,
Shrugs off the darker dawn,
For this ukase from London
Binds all within its thrall.

Our rulers earnestly do strive
To labour for the common good.
And Whitehall prescience decides
The best for vassals such as us.
So, willing and unwilling,
Must we then all conform,
The business man, the dreamer,
The old fold all forlorn;
And with both sick and healthy
Tread forth the human path,
We mixtures of variety
Will be as one at last.

So bravely let us not repine,
But face our cold, wet summertime.

Fair Play for Dinosaurs

Give a thought, I pray, for the dinosaurs,
All those swamps, savannas and fearful storms;
Each day endless hours foliage feeding
To fill vast bulks, needful, depressing.
Never music of flutes to soothe savage breasts,
Just pterodactyl's screech at tree-top's height;
Stealthy sounds every night precludes gentle sleep,
Reptiles nocturnal prowl undergrowth deep.
Let us picture a pair of huge dinosaurs,
Plus a brood: (sweet little teeth, small dinky claws).
Dad must then guard, always steadfast and true,
A ponderous mum, the little ones too.
Worries and dangers to crowd his poor brain;
Fierce neighbours, foul weather, and awful terrain.
Think kindly, I beg on all dinosaurs,
They've had a bad press all down the long years.

Little Emma

An Emma small, 'afore the dawn,
To wintry Scottish darkness born,
Emergent as a budding rose,
Her limbs as fair as petals shown.

And Halley's comet, speeding high,
Does now the new-born babe espy,
Unable to arrest his flight
He brighter grows in rare delight.
The deep hushed ward awakes to life,
Quick flitting forms cross pools of light,
As muted moths they flutter round,
Not anxious, but in duty bound.

Then nature's dawn, in chastened plight,
Fast hastens to dismiss the night,
Guides lancet rays of morning grace
To greet, illume, small Emma's face.

Slim mother Dawn, a queen arrayed,
In pillowed ease her babe displays;
And all about the new-grown light
Shows busy staff at nursing rites.

Let not this brave occasion go
Until, unless, there takes a bow

The adjunct father, hesitant,
Yet now assured to great content.

And further back, by melting shores,
Soft tread the dim progenitors;
A human chain, springs and summer,
From cave's recess to little Emma.

The Box

Oh television innocence,
Oh days of back and white,
Of no repeats continuance,
When wrong was seldom right.

When planners weird were not the fashion,
Nor private grief filmed for a cheque,
When pleasantness received expression
In equal measure to distress.

When porn and bosoms only showed
But twice a week as there we sat;
And uncombed locks and unwashed beards
Were not *de rigueur* for each act.

Our news time mirror on the world,
The clarity of misery.
Fresh corpses sleeping unperturbed
Dream on in deep felicity.

Oh, dear lost days of long ago,
Oh, television crouching there,
Could you but me a button show
Which switches back to yesteryear.

Ode to M&S Lemon Sponge

Ah, Marks and Spencer, though hast made
A sweet as fair as Helen's face,
An truly light as fairies' wings,
In pastel shade of daffodils,
Of honey taste, Hymettus bees,
Hither borne on Attice breeze.
A taste for gods. Olympus feast,
Or kitchen table, family treat.
This dish must equal pleasure give
To Labour or Conservative,
Let Arab and let Jew unite
To eat as one in shard delight.
Let Ruskies, Yanks, in friendship dine
And reach agreement o'er the wine;
Soothed hearts and minds shall content be
By stomachs eased to harmony.
And so, word wide, may there be found
Store shelves stacked high with M.S sponge,

Well done Marks, and well done Spencer,
In double toil thou toiled together
Produced this food, this fine confection,
A packaged dish in fresh perfection;
And greater men have lesser wrought,
In longer labour less brought forth
But thou hast strove with keener mind,

Thou benefactors of mankind;
Now careful housewives make your choice,
And husbands, children all rejoice,
Thus, though the world be full of gloom,
Yet gleams a light – the lemon sponge.

Pale Shade of Hope

Oh, my elusive Littlewoods,
Since long, long ago;
Sought thee have I in your fortune's wood
Since forty years ago.
My crosses stand there all in vain,
Corroding in the winter rain
Since countless years ago.

From forecast charts, by pin-struck chance,
Slow careful thought or lightning glance,
The long years nothing shows
Hope sinks low each year that goes.

British or Aussie, the season's flow
Through long, lost years ago,

Yet with worn hand, with rheumy eye,
Shall I persist until I die;
And coffin laid will count the cost,
Of all those entries, money lost,
Since long, long ago.

Hough for Starters

"First catch your hough" says Mrs Beaton,
'When you have it can be eaten'.

But, asking here within your kitchen,
"What is a hough, dear Mrs Beaton?".

Does it walk, or does it fly,
In the wide, blue Scottish sky?

But soft, hear we not a gentle cough,
From yon gentle hough on yonder buff?

And surely 'tis unkind to shoot,
Until one has been introduced?

Dear Mrs B, if you'll excuse me,
I'll pass the hough writ on your menue.

And start at once on good roast beef,
With sprouts, potatoes, all complete.

At Lughton Inn, please leave out hough,
Your starters show a choice enough.

And all the nice and cheery diners,
Can work their way through all the courses.

Let peace and mercy fill our minds
This Christmas as we drink and dine.

Let's leave the hough to safely fly,
In the wide blue Scottish sky.

Siren's Song

Why here remain these winter days
When I might be so far away?
With Spain's gold sun full on my face,
Blue skies by tall palms interlaced,
These pensioned, old and creaking bones
For rheumic pains a fitting home,
Should easeful rest in warmer clime
And move, perhaps, to supply style.
The seasons garlic, olive, grape,
My blood enrich to healthier state.
A small white house, long cloudless days
By gleaming sands and gentle waves.
Hard earned retirements soft solace,
Expatriate without disgrace.
But stay awhile, methinks this seems
A spider's web of airy dreams,
Where orange groves and warmth and wine
With Seville sunsets are entwined,
And red Alhambra's moorish halls
Hear not muezzin's upraised calls,
These gossamers of wishful thought
Wherein are strands of fancy caught,
All sober prudence thrusts aside
And cool reflection doth deride,
Spain's sirens sing a sweet refrain,
Yet heart and mind still here remain,

Deaf to allure I'll stay beside
Humber's wide and muddy tide.

King's Town-upon-Hull

Dear delectable Hull on the Hull,
Bright Jewel of the Northern Crown;
Where Humber's tidal flow anoint
The muddy nose of Sammy's Point.
And silver-winged seagulls
Soar high o'er Rank's tower'd mill;
Old Harbour winds a liquid snake
By Wincolmlee, where barges wait,
Laden deep to chug to Goole;
A grim, grey place, but that's the rule.
Freeboard awash they wallow on
Indifferent to the Siren's song,
Who on Reed's Island comb their hair
And fixed smile to hide despair;
Far, far from Cyclades rocky isles
And Grecian lads and Attic smiles.

A street, the Land of Green ginger
Crooked lifts an age-old finger
To welcome you to cobbled ways
Laid for ancient stage-coach days;
And thence to bustling Whitefriargate,
Where shoppers spend at spendthrift pace.
In tree-lined suburbs better types
Graceful live their better lives.
In western Hull, near Cottingham,

Delight and daffodils abound.
The people there they keep apart
From high-rise flats and coarser parts.
Should you now long to visit here,
Deliberate with the greatest care;
It may not be a pleasant change
For folks round here are nobbut strange.
They dubious view with gloomy face
Those not native to this place,
Far better far to go to Leeds,
Now there's a town that's bound to please.

A Lada am I

I come from haunts of smoke and grime,
Conceived in clangour, Marxist style;
In noise and dust and Russian oaths
To replace dreams of Russian hopes,
No lullaby, no cradle song
Did ease my childhood soft along.
For born full-grown was square-shaped me,
As Venus was from out the sea
Above my head steel girders high,
Above her head the bright blue sky.
The Godfathers were close at hand,
Observers of two separate strands;
One sad; a grey and lined foreman,
(Worn victim of a 5-year plan)
And boisterous, moody Poisdon,
Whose breasts the creamy seas along,
The first must guide production lines,
And strive to evade Moscow's fines;
The other rules th' Aegean waves,
And sometimes hapless seamen saves,
The Old, the New, pursue two ways,
Divergent as their differing days.
Both formal hold, as a banner,
One a trident, one a spanner.
They friends would be, could they but know,
The way frail chance has linked them so.

So here am I at factory gate,
In helpless, passive, patient wait.
My destination known to those
Who sit in Kremlin's dark enclose;
And devious delved their turgid minds
To ensnare innocent Mankind.
Can they a field of turmoil till
The harvest grist shall fill their mill.
They say, let's send to island England
Those Lada cars for them to ride in.
Thus foreign currency we ear,
And English sterling never spurn,
We'll earnest tell that fog-bound land
These cars were made by eager hands
Of Russians, care-free, strong and true,
(You choose the shade, red, white or blue)
So buy our cars, we plead you should,
To further world-wide brotherhood.
Let Russia lead, Red Star, the light
'Neath which the nations shall unite
And forward march, all ranks in step,
Drilled, rationed and apportioned rest,
All equal are in numbered drafts,
Except of course, Headquarters Staff.

Still wait I here, this Lada I
The scribblers write while I here sigh,

But now at last, a train, a train;
To bear me off to places strange,
In safety, not in spirit, chained.
Across a vast unending plain
To chase the sun, but ne're to gain,
Steppes and forest, lakes and trees,
'Tis all delight for me to see,
Onwards swaying through the night,
A myriad stars in blue-black sight.
This iron serpent clanking plods
Past Minsk and Pinsk and Novgorod,
And all is peace and nought is sad
In gentle drive to Leningrad.
'Till breathing, jerking, half-asleep,
See a stone – set quay, a proud, fine ship,
To make my heart in wonder skip
And outward leap past gaunt cranes blight
To where the Baltic sparkles bright,
Ah, Ulysses! As thou I'll be
And fearlessly shall cross the sea;
No whales, sea monsters, sudden storms
Shall they deter what'er befalls,
These wastes of tumbling, foaming waves
Shall never be my watery grave.
With North Star on our starboard beam
The captain stands at radar screen
Whose circling finger scans the night
Until Old England hoves in sight,

East Anglia's low and sandy shore
Where sea fights land for evermore.

Events go on and now I'm sold
A college man, or so I'm told.
He's rather short, not old, not young,
A well-used mould, just anyone;
But as he's short, he wears high heels
To overlook those shorter still,
His residence is Golders Green
(Golder himself is never seen)
He Sunday wears a Russian hat
To talk to other Labour chaps.
They noble-browed blueprint a world
Where Peace and Joy rule undisturbed
He's kind, contentious, oftimes boring
Hooked on day-dreams skywards soaring,
Yet him, I will not criticise
For most my wants are satisfied.
He cossets me with fond attention
As though his child get his affection,
No servant man could ever be
Content, secure, as happy me.
I think the Russians splendid chaps
Spread all over their great map.
But England is the place for me
And no place else I'd want to be,
Deep roots have I in England grown,

This is my land, my very own;
And when I'm old, as scrap I'd rather
Be reborn a Ford Fiesta.

The Efelant

It has a wise old face, a trunk for a nose
Which it waves up and down wherever it goes.
It has a great thick body, round thick legs,
How can it curl up when it goes to bed?
From a Granddad head grown huge floppy ears
Quite enough to wipe away tears.
Do efelants cry? I expect they do
Except when they're old (and solemn too).
Are young ones o-bee-jent to Mum and Dad?
Like eating up sprouts and not being bad,
They say that efelants never forget,
So how easy to learn the al-fa-bet.
I don't like snakes, they slither and slide.
And under my bed might secretly hide,
But an efelant now, I'd be safe with him,
For he's steady and strong, not slimy and slim,
With an efelant friend, what fun to stay
All night 'till the sun drives the stars away.

A Faraway Place

North of Watford, a thousand miles
From Cockney voice and London grime,
Dreaming by Humber's ceaseless tide,
Flowing deep and flowing wide,
Estuary banks but few feet o'er,
Flat and low-spread as Holland's shore
Lies Hull, clean, modern and ancient,
City and County by Royal Patent
Kingston-on-Hull, the river Hull
A brown serpent winds, slow and dull,
Bridged six times to stitch the town,
Bank-side warehouses frowning down,
A township by King Edward planned
As port and fortress for his land,
A shield to guard the Northern Sea
On land stern role, the bloom of peace,
A town grown out in green fields reach,
Beyond the farms a white capped beach,
A Humber Bridge for present prides,
A Folly's debt for future times,
Around in sprawling, kindly Hull,
From Wilcolmlee and Dairycoates,
From Derringham and Spring Bank West
Go, sturdy, independent folk
By other places unimpressed,

Down Blackfriargate the stony sets
Seen mostly fit for monks cabots;
But Whitefriargate, why that's the road
Which Marks and suchlike make their own,
And here the busy shoppers throng;
A homely place where all belong;
The high-browed chap, his broad-beamed wife,
A way-out youth to add a spice,
And some there be, a feckless stream,
Whose thoughts are born on telly's screen:
With fivers burning hot in purse
Strive for that state they secret nurse.
But let us leave this madding crowd
Where once grave friars praying bowed.
Land of Green Ginger's narrow lane,
Hushed in silence points the way
To Drypool's contradictory name
Where trees and church and grave remain
All old and gnarled, the dried-out pond
Is gone, and silent stays the burial ground.
Away along the Hedon road
Lies Marfleet's marshy, asthmic cold.
A weed-grown sluggish stream does creep
Dejectedly to Hedon Creek,
And thence with gurgling sighs outgoes
To drown itself in Humber's flows
Where plaintive gulls, thin streaks of sound,
Against an evening sky abound.

Here, as the air fills up with dark,
I, and my humble song, depart.

Soliloquy Before Walking to the Village

To shave or not to shave? That is the question,
Whether 'tis better to remove, firm with razor blade
And creamed brush, those bristles white
(Sad signals of old age decays) from off the chin
So as to show, in resemblance slight,
A faded image of a once smooth skin,
A visage scraped, unshielded, bare,
Full exposed to northern sharp edged air.
Or, despising all proud neighbours looks,
Unshaved to sally forth, a natural sage,
Bedecked in nature's truest state.
Perchance as would from woodland hermitage
Shyly go a forest man, on thinnest gruel fed
And beech nuts hard, a crooked staff in hand,
Along the leafy lanes, head bowed, avoiding all,
Self inward shrunk 'gainst shrill-cried taunts

And yet, and yet, why should those village eyes be feared?
If bristles be the sprouting seeds of trim Shakespearean
Beard
My troubled thoughts go round, revolve within thy brain.
I'll not go out, nor shave; it looks like rain.

She Sits in Pensive Melancholy

A gentle light, an evening land,
At table's edge my pale white hand,
The hand which raised off china plate
Carved slices from a carcased fate,
Cro-Magnon squatting by his kill,
Myself arrayed in fancy frill,
At dusk the hunter with his prey,
Myself has dined at fade of day —
We comrades are.
Wan solace comes in misty thought —
All ants and kings will end as naught;
So humans, cattle, creatures all,
Each one obeys his final call,
And drops away, received in soil,
Is mingled, mixed, in earthly coil,
All hid from sight, all hid away,
While worms make fresh the old decay.

Claremont House

The house is half hid by a ring of tall trees,
As guardsman they stand in fresh morning's breeze
And high overhead white clouds sail by
On a vast blue sea as their journeys they ply.
Fronting the house are gardens as one may expect.
There inside the house are folks grown old.
The frail, the halt, the sick and the slow,
All wounded by the shafts of life.
But here at peace from tempests strife.

Indeed, tall trees shade a noble house
And noble the cause therein espoused.
Residents and staff do here combine
By differing styles their status define.
Here Jackie's the Chief, perceptive and wise,
And the carers a team who kind care do provide,
The sun may shine or storms may blow,
But the house maintains its steadfast pose.
While the blooms in the gardens appear as fair maids
Their glowing small faces brightly displayed.

In fancy compared to a ship at sea,
A fine tall ship on an ocean breeze.
While Captain Jackie on the bridge controls
Both the crew and the frail on deck and below.

The ship is well-found, the crew brave and bold,
And on the ship's log all facts must be told,
The vessel sails on, by day and by night,
A course set by the stars with the stars shining bright.
The masters at east when a landfall is called
From the foredeck watch to all on board.
With the ship safe in harbour it is time to leave
The remembered scents of the infinite sea.

The human fate is but to die
And frail humankind must by fate comply.
So Charon calls here as at all other places
And here does his task as he must without traces.
At midnight hour no faint foot-fall
As pale-faced Charon comes to call.
No oaken door can bar his way
No iron key his hand forbade.
By the River Styx his boat awaits
And the rest is hidden by misted Fate.

The tale is now told, the House is at rest,
And the Fates will decide that which is best.
On the sky's blue arc silent clouds go
To far-away lands I never shall know.

A Gastronomic Stroll Through Yorkshire Parts

In far-off, cheerful Beverley
Is widely purchased celery.

But in sad Hull is fish,
An often chosen dish.

Down in busy Market Weighton
Becomes boiled mutton gravely eaten.

At banquets held at Castle Howard
By noble lords is venison devoured.

While at Millington and Frodingham
They feed their men on cheese and ham.

In Thorton-le-Dale and Wharram-le-Street
Old Frenchmen there take garlic with meat.

At Euston Parva, descendants of Rome
Chew stringy goat and dream of home.

In slumb'rous Holne-on-Spalding Moor
Are pheasants sold at darkened doors.

The curving lure of Crescent Cave
Is worthy of its noted fame.

In strong-walled famous York
The Vikings there eat lots of pork.

There Shepherd's Stew and Ploughman's Pie
Are cooked in good old English style.

In Cherry Burton, 'neath the oaks
County types eat roasted ducks.

At Burton Agnes on the wolds
For tea 'tis scrambled eggs and scones.

At Swanland, from the village pond,
Geese are cooked, but rarely swans.

In Cottingham, in glassy show,
Fat Dutchmen red tomatoes grown.

The Land of Nod, a hamlet of dreams
Where dreamers eat mushrooms and drink harebell tea.

In Driffield where glum people live
Farm workers there eat lots of pig.

Rural vicars, in white surplice
All dine well on farming surplus.

Here where the tides of Humber flow
The folks have varied tastes you know.

So now my little song is sung
My leave I'll take and I'll be gone.

Cottingham's Sun

Season of wasps and sun's ascendancy,
Of cloudless skies and browning leaves,
The rainless days are hope's duplicity,
We walk dry-foot where the Humber has been.

All fields are bare from the gathered harvest,
No more green shoots will grace the spring,
The earth lies cracked and dry, defenceless,
Shall Skidby's tall windmill collapse on its hill?

Village folk flock along to sweet St Mary's,
And the Rector there prays for rain's return.
By Beverley's Councils' sombre Sessions
Are fears in white beards duly confirmed.

Wood pigeons call not from Eppleworth woods,
Down Castle Hill road no traffic now flows,
The people have fled, in igloos to dwell,
They dream as they sit, midst white arctic snows.

Hope and Fear

In last dying breath shall my spirit take flight
From the grey shrouded form lying still.
Sightless eyes cannot see ascent to the skies,
Through cloud to the stars, gleaming beacons in space,
Leaving empty, abandoned, a mortal estate.
By questing hope borne shall I soar to the dream time,
To my Maker's soft drifting dream time,
The flowing dream tides of Heaven,
Silently lapping remote astral shores.
In far stellar spaces join those resurrected,
Earthly hosts risen, in eternal quiescence.

Yet in distant far galaxies may menace abide,
As sombre worlds turn 'neath pallid grey skies.
Other gods, other forces, may there have their being,
Malignant and merciless, watching and waiting.
A universe stirring, erupting to bear
Emanation of evil, spreading cosmic despair.

Ode to the minced beef of Old England

In a rich brown gravy reclining,
Before me displayed for my dining,
Minced beef, no less, of old England,
Thus the heart of a nation is signalled.

This sea-girt island embalmed
As a jewel begirt by its shores,
While others, like Frenchmen, distressed,
Bound to Europe, enchained in unrest.

But here, at high noon, is perceived
A full platter of nourishing feed,
Potatoes and cabbage in heaps,
And silence doth reign as we eat.

Of Agincourt and Alamein
We sing the pride of England's fame,
But praise is long tine overdue
To brave minced beef in English stew.

With sturdy limb and rosy cheek
Our children child-like pleasures seek,
At school they drink at learning's cup,
Refreshed, the life force welling up.

The sun shall shine o'er golden fields,
The midnight moon cast silvered gleams
On midday plates minced beef shall flow,
And put to flight our transient flow.

To Belt or Not to Belt

Proud Britons never shall be slaves,
At least until these 'belt up' days;
But now, distraught, I sit entrapped,
Reflecting on dear freedoms past.
This law-abiding hapless I
Alone cannot the law defy;
Robbers, scoundrels, most escape
Retribution's just embrace.

Yet belt-less I police would seize
And thence to dungeons deep proceed
To cast inside a felon's cell
Where to dark walls I'd tearful tell
My mournful tale. The stifled air
Would close around with anxious fear
Of justice grim to come.

The Magistrate is seated high,
Enthroned above poor cringing I
Who listens to his words in awe
His winged words – in flight they soar
To reach, resound, from arching roof,
Reciting in oppressive proof
My heinous crime.

Against the laws of this our land
You wretched person, there you stand
Most guilty found. Oh sinful one

Let justice now be swiftly done;
A hundred pounds, licence endorsed,
This sentence does our court enforce
For heinous crime.

'Tis said a car, but fleeting seen,
Has driver close resembling me,
Who belt-less sits, a fearless knight
Defiant of the laws full might;
A shining brown, a visage brave,
Unshackled, calm and unafraid.
My dopple-ganger thus redeems
Valour for my nascent dreams.

The Abandoned Village

An iron bridge, a river's flow,
And high above a vast, still sky,
No human treads the fields below,
In dreams the soundless years go by.

The soundless years, the dreams unknown,
The pallid shapes, bereft of song.
And sped away with those long flown
A stray old man, whose task is done.

Unknown Shore

Pervasive melancholy comes with age,
Steals to my side and takes my hand -
The wings of the morning are fled far away,
Heavy my paths in a hedged-about land.

Now a companion have I for slow turning days
To go by the long evening shore:
To tread stony sands where the grey surging sea
Sweeps away in deep tides all years gone before.

And the travell'd bright hills lie far, far behind -
Here at hand waits the somber sea:
A voyage to make whence none have returned,
Nor shall my melancholy and me.

Perchance the surf creams on a soft gleaming shore
Far beyond any mapped earthly land.
Can I haven find there in peace past compare,
Heart's ease on far distant strand?

So many set out, not one has returned
Through abyss of night from across the great sea.
The terror of tempests, of perils unknown;
What hope can there be for all such as me?

Untouched may the shore be for all evermore,
And never a craft reach the strand.
Deep lost all who journey: down, down to seas floor -
Far, far out of sight of that land.

In soft summer airs does a silence dream on
O'er a mystic and silver-shored strand?
For the faintest of echoes has never returned
From the deeps, or the shores, of a far away land.

The Mystic Fir Tree

They are there; both Haley and I
Know this to be certain and true.
Other people just glance and go by
Unseeing: if only they knew!

Their pale sight sees but a fir tree
Leaning close to a house's side.
But Haley and I, we see and perceive
A blending of shapes which others deride.

Here hide two ghosts who bravely escaped
From a dungeon atop Castle Hill.
Entombed they had lain and despaired,
Darkly enclosed, pallid and ill.

And the Lord of the Goblins, - he
Who had cast them in durance vile,
Was determined they'd evermore be
Detained, enchained; 'neath the Castle's ruined pile.

In blue skies on high the wheeling birds flew
O'er two wraiths in a cell, clamp'd and still.
Harvest folk toiled nearby, but none of them knew,
Not even the miller of Skidby windmill.

Lock'd underground, mask'd from the sun's sky,
Thinner and thinner they wasted each day,

But then they did find, that with a great try,
From their chains, these shrunk waifs, could slip quite
away.

Under scattered stars nebulous light,
In the gaze of a beady-eyed vole,
'Neath the black velvet blanket of night,
Through bars away, away they stole.

Freedom enchanted, yet needs must they hide
From the Lord of the Goblins, - who
With his minions would search far and wide -
He was cruel and wicked: well this they knew.

On Cottingham Green they found a ladder,
Propped it up, in a close, to a house's side,
Clamber'd up; to king Night a pleas didst proffer,
And lo! - Here's a leaning fir tree at a house's side!
Soft hours slide by in sunshine and rain,
The Lord of the Goblins seeks high and low;
But him they regard with cool disdain,
Observing the rage of a thwarted foe.

Contented they taste the honey-sweet airs,
And sip at the nectar'd dew,
And for extra nourishment repair
To nibble a beech nut or two.

Summers do fade and winters must flee,
In each seasons sequented lays;
Two ghosts on a ladder, disguised as a tree,
In sanctum shall dream pensive dream-times away.

The Intrepid Traveler

The voyager sets boldly forth,
From kith and kin a sad farewell,
Shall gallantry be brought to naught?
The Fates themselves cannot foretell.

The banks and braes o' Scotland brave
Fall swift behind the speeding wheels -
Ahead the goal, damp crescent caves,
Where elders two a vigil keep.

The way is long; high mountain peaks
Assail the sky in solemn style,
And round their base the roadway creeps
Where fiery dragons crouching hide.

And unicorns and beastly boars
Within the wooded slopes abound
To seek out travelers to devour,
Especially young and tender ones.

Through all these dangers, ice and snow,
O'er barren moors, by strange defiles,
The thundering chariot thrusting goes
And leaves behind the lonely miles.

Intent upon her task is she,
With precious chart she navigates,
Like steadfast mariners at sea
In fixèd gaze doth concentrate.

A passenger she hath besides,
A fragile princess all declare,
Who on a mini throne presides.
And there anoints the enclosed air.

In Pennine parts the Yorkshire types,
Unwashed, uncouth and savage are,
From wattle huts they sally forth,
Hurl rocks and curses at the car.

She ponders as the hours go by:
- 'Tis hard to reach sweet Ithaca,
But Ulysses' bold daughter I,
And I a mirror'd portraiture. -

But now a ray, the low red sun
Beaming light from horizon pours;
The traveler near her haven comes,
The evening scene is a second dawn.

By Skidby Hill and Castle Road
She sees ahead the crescent caves,
And valour is its own reward,
And quiet the inward spirit lays.

(77)

This song is sung and silence reigns,
The heroine reflects her day,
And darkness all the earth pervades,
The minstrel softly steals away.

A Plea

Then do we breathe celestial airs
Spun off from swift-revolving spheres?
Our living, growing soil, each day
Enriched, nurtured by cosmic rays?
Is there some firm, all-seeing eye
That watches each until they die
A human death; then swept from earth
To timeless duties, astral cares?
Thus are we all and every one
Immortal? - yet tied to services to come,
And never rest, be never laid
In deep, dark comfort of the grave,
We pray to Heaven for saving grace,
A quiet grave in a peaceful place;
Both husk and spirit there interr'd,
Repose, reflection, 'neath the stars.

Doubtful Journey

In this, this melancholy May,
Shall Autumn come before the Spring,
And waiting Summer drift away
Ere springlike days are ushered in?
For far beyond bare Pennine hills,
By Lancashire's grey misted dells
Do crouching lurk grim Winter's chills,
Cold fronts and isobaric spells.

So careful think upon your plan
To visit these bleak northern parts,
Let courage with wise caution join
And ponder whether you should start.
If you then up the M1 dare,
Car anti-freeze already mixed,
Snug clad in thermal underwear,
Use lesser speed to lessen risk.

No flags, I fear, will welcome fly,
When you your yokels 'Hurrah' cry,
Nor village church bells loudly ring.
Yet igloo seven will open wide,
Affection greet you there inside....
Beyond the windows frosts still cling,
Dead daffodils where no birds sing.

Spring Sonnet

(With apologies to Wordsworth)

Season of crocus, rate bills and rain,
A pallid-cheeked sun which rarely prevails.
Season of frosts and flowers long dead,
Humans in thermal underwear clad.
Season of jolly jobbing workmen
Risen refreshed from hibernation....
Bare straggled hedges, moss covered lawn,
The rose bed a waste of ruins forlorn;
Sad rusted shears in garden shed wait,
A poor worn mower still not replaced.
The fuchsia is mildewed, the cuckoo sings
A querulous note to hasten Spring -
That Nymph, a'flutter with whimsy airs,
Gay and capricious, fleet and fair;
Carelessly gracious, who sometimes delights,
Who rests amongst bright stars at night....
Wood pigeons coo from dell and from copse,
And dear small birds eat primula tops.
Shy snowdrops hand as pendant pearls,
To innocent gaze at the close brown earth....
Gonvolvulus and celandine
With honeysuckle intertwined
Once in springtime hedgerow grew,
Not now, not now, th're lost to view.
Mechanical diggers grubbed them out,

Those hedges poets wrote about,
And that is why you'll see them not,
Young funeral-named forget-me-nots.
Dug up are hedges from country roads,
To fatten the profit the farmer holds,
More acres of soil, a prairie plain,
More golden wheat, more golden gain....
Sweep o'er the land, o'er hill and dale,
Dismiss nymph Spring, bid her depart,
And let thy rays melt winter hearts.

High Thoughts

In a copse of angled igloos
A man, on a ladder, there paints;
His thoughts, in free air, are diffused;
His feet, metal-runged, are constrained

Wood pigeons soft coo in near trees,
The tundra lies not there below,
But silk wheat rape yellow fields,
Whose profit, unsown, was well known.

Rural District Council dustmen
Clatter away with fine zeal,
Clearing tins, packets and cartons,
The debris of country folks meals.

This painter, high on his ladder
Looks out, as a king, o'er the land;
Pedestall'd there in raised splendour
While neighbours, as pygmies, low stand.

To the postman passing on cycle
Gives he a most kind regal wave.
In delusions of grandeur impanell'd,
From such how shall he be saved?

The Vicar sits high on his steeple,
One arm round the cross to be safe,

Looks down at the shoppers, his people,
His flock, who from worship oft stray.

The clouds touch his head in their passing,
They bless the bald pate as they go;
The rooks flutter down to damp grasses
To commune at tombstones below.

So up on the spire of St. Mary's,
At the rooftops along Harland Rise,
Two men with purpose disparate
View each other in startled surprise.

Closer to Heaven, the cleric aspires,
On thin rungs desp'rately climbed.
The other, early of mundane desires,
Alas, now to madness declines.

Then both hear a far off droning,
See an aeroplane crossing the sky,
Both think of the pilot there flying,
Both think, 'Could he but be I'.

The Smile

Oh dearest Mr Gorbachoff,
How long before that smile wears off?
How long before a Kremlin frown
Dispenses gloom the world around?
And Raisa of the sable fur?
(Which few of Russian women wear),
Her smile may fade, expression set,
At serving maids in Budapest.
The guards patrolling Leningrad,
Are they happy? are they sad?
Trudging up the Nevski Prospekt,
Sternly warning merry moujiks,
Counting ice floes on the Neva,
Can all this add up to pleasure?
Yet thinking of their own Great Man,
Then his smile must surely cheer them.
But not, I think, refusenik Jews
Exiled to Siberian snows.
Toiling by the barbed wire fences,
Nightly crowded in dim hutments,
Mirth and merriment are absent,
Dragg'd despair, a constant present.
Away in Kabul, Mr Gorbachoffe,
Perchance your rating slips somewhat.
Do Afgan corpses often smile

Lying prone on mountain side?
Where napthalm is the only leaven
Raining down from friendship's heaven.
Hard minds are swift and deeds are sharp,
Beguiling words may soften hearts....
Oh wily Mr Gorbachoff,
Your smile's a mask, please take it off.

The White Cat

In shadow'd garden, darken'd field,
'Neath clouded moon or star-cast sky,
A killer ruthless power wields
O'er piteous prey marked out to die.

The white cat hides by hedge and bush,
A silent shadow, grey and blurred.,
With flattened crouch, then flashing rush
Strikes timorous mouse and hapless bird.

In darkest night are dark deeds wrought
By tearing talons, outstretched wide.
The hunter has the hunted caught,
The victims have in terror died.

The crumpled wing of bloodied bird,
The mouse's ripped and reddened form,
Both have an anguished ending shared
In deepest shade, in airs forlorn.

No more shall joyous fluting note
From one bird's throat in sweetness call.
One mouse no more twitch nervous nose,
His body lies 'gainst garden wall.

Two tiny threads in nature's web,
Two minutes flecks on earth's vast globe;

Each have their frail existence led,
And each fulfilled a destined role.

Now sun's new rays disperse dark night,
Guide in a hushed and tranquil dawn,
Reveals red roses to the sight
Of fair and fragrant, spacious morn.

The house reflects the warming sun,
A door is opened, welcome wide;
The child stands calling for her pet
"Where are you Heide? Come, dear Heid":

With feline grace the pure white cat,
So stately strolls across the lawn,
Accepts the milk bowl on the mat
And drinks; with thoughtful mien then yawns.
The child sits stroking on her lap
Her winsome-faced and silken cat,
Who sweetly mews,
And softly purrs;
Wrapped round with comfort, drowsy, sighs,
And closes yellow killer eyes.

Morning Speculations

The rough gravelled path lies hedge in with bushes,
Through sun's golden shafts morning mists rise
                               dispersing.
As my slow wand'ring steps pass dew-heavy rushes
Come clearly repeat notes of a blackbird rehearsing.

This abandoned old lane is a pattern of life,
The path my feet tread reflects my true living.
Would I welcome its close at yon blue-shaded skyline,
At barrier of thorns at farthest sights edge?
Marking the place where the rutted trail closes,
Setting the hour when life's journey will end.

Long ages ago was this path a swift highway?
Busy with movement at noon's thronged array.
Long ago was this man in his eager bright years,
Youthful and strong, a stranger to fears?
But times winters have furrowed, worn both to decay,
Times summers restore not by oft-shown display.

High above anchored fields another world circles,
Remote and unsullied, serene and aloof,
Floating free on blue oceans of heaven's wide spaces
Sail drifting cloud islands and far mountain ranges.
Does the Lord of Creation from deep fathoms of silence,

Coldly regard, with transcedental wisdom,
Observant, percipient, detached and uncaring,
Man's evils and follies, his hopes and sad yearning?

The Adversaries

"This submarine (U.630) had been launched a year
previously at the Blohm and Voss yard in Hamburg and
was under the command of Oberleutnant zur See Werner
Winkler, a native of Wilhelmshaven, who was just short
of his 28th birthday".

'THE MONTH OF THE LOST U-BOATS'.
By Geoffrey Jones.

Oberleutnant Werner Winkler,
By Wilhelmshaven born and bred;
Each day a boyhood beach to wander -
But now no more, for Werner's dead.

Sydney Simpson, war reservist,
At Wells-on-Sea was born and bred:
Navy listed, forty, grey haired,
Sydney lives, but Werner's dead.

Work-worn corvette, madly tossing
On the wide Atlantic wastes -
Slides a U-boat, sombre, lurking,
Torpedoes set for instant race.
On the corvette, Sydney Simpson,

Seaman, first-class, able-bodied,
Pull his levers, depth charge swiftly
Rises, tumbles, dread and solid.

Turns and tumbles, falls and shatters,
A thunder's roar on U'boats head,
Crashes, splinters, kills and fractures -
The sea boils on, but Werner's dead.

Metals, bodies, sink deep spaces,
Above them heaves the white-capp'd seas,
Batteries, tubes and grey, blind faces,
Dark fathoms low their grave to be.

High above, a tense search keeping,
Huddles Sydney, eyes rimmed red.
Oceans deep is Werner sleeping,
Limp and quiet, his problems fled.

Sydney, off watch, weary, grimy,
Eats his sausage, mash and bread,
Sucks mugged tea, sweet and steaming,
Bank eyes fixed at steel bulkhead.

Werner died and Sydney living,
Yet to meet in Heaven's space -
What will be their style of greeting,
Strife-lined foemen, face to face?

Debris floating from the wreckage,
Jacket, wallet, photos, letters,
Garnered for Their Lordships' records -
Crewmen gaze at Werner's image.

Childless Sydney stares intently,
'Till memory holds, ne'er to dim
The face of Werner, frank and friendly;
That trusting smile meant just for him.

The grinding war at last is ended -
No heroes' flags at Wells-on-Sea
Where Sydney, vague, gentle and agéd,
A pebbl'd shore walks, discharged and free.

———————————

The sea ever changes and stays the same,
Always the beach as it was remains.
But Sydney, of course, is now quite mad,
For he talks to a son he never had.

Werner dead and Sydney living,
Human flotsam sunk and sinking,
Grief and pain and storm-cast seas,
Pale dreams of hope for haven's peace.

The shining bowl of Heaven's sky
Is mirror'd wide for mortal eye,

And does, at morn, some fresh-sprung beam
Refract a golden haven's gleam?

On Seeing an Old Photograph

Oh child, oh fresh-faced child,
Thou cannot be this grey and lined old man
In whom are age and melancholy joined,
And thou so light-foot on they rainbow span.
Between us lies an abyss of lost years,
Through which has flowed forgotten days,
A stream of time in distant oceans drowned.
I look across the gulf at thee,
Thou should not look at me -
Thy wide-eyed gaze would only see
Thyself, as thou will surely be.

Hornsea Beach

Across the flat alluvial plain,
Where cows and corn and farmers reign,
'Tis eighteen miles to Hornsea beach;
Then England stops. A shelving reach,
Contested by the grey North Sea,
Is sometimes land and sometimes sea.
Here waves forever win and lose
In forward surge, retreating hiss:
The tides do strive for evermore
On turmoil'd sandy, pebbl'd shore.

Loud sound the thund'rous hooves
In winter's storms:
Soft run small wavelets smooth
At summer's dawns,
Throughout continuous years
The curling wavecrests rear....
The wearied strand
Is outpost land.

Voiceless people wander the beach,
Strident gulls wheel high in sky's reach -
The folk drift along to become black dots,
And gulls fly afar until they are lost,
The years slide away, then they too are gone,
Time vanish'd steals back and sees the same sun.

Past fierce and fair-haired Angles,
Past tall and dreadful Danes,
Who once were here,
Unseen, they are near:
Lost souls from out of the past,
By perplex'd sadness possessed.
In sky's mirror they seek banish'd days
For sunlight long clouded away.
They are wraiths of mist by the shore,
Shadows, pale cast, of times before;
These ghosts from the land
Drifts slow on the strand;
Searching they stare to the sea
For longships that never can be...
As for me, I sit by the sea,
Thinking on men I never shall see,
Nor times long ago. Deep I sigh,
Swift returned gulls give raucous reply.

The evening sun is red and low,
Night's cloak hands near, 'tis time to go.
May Angles, Danes, an auric haven find,
Calm airs and quietude of mind...
Now Hornsea beach deserted stands,
Murmuring sea and silent sands;
From here no motorway to home,
But B roads only, as I know.
The fading light long shadows cast

On darker hedgerows as I pass.
In western sky last gold retreats,
By field and coppice blackness creeps;
All cows and farmers are at rest
Upon the plain of Holderness.

Birthday Thoughts

No savour find I now in life,
My bones are worn, my stray hair white.
I do not walk but creak along,
Youth's suppleness far lost and gone.
Yet curiosity's the key
Which holds, supports, this breathless me
The solemn grave must vacant wait
Until my int'rest doth abate
In Maggie, Scargill and McGregor
Circling round in dance macabre
Joined by Kinnock and McGahey,
Storm-troop pickets, other lackeys;
Helped by papers and the box,
Stirr'd up daily, piping hot.
Miners, policemen's confrontations,
Scrums and charges, accusations,
Speeches, ploys and protestations,
Strategems and aspirations;
A serial drama, thrilling, true,
I cannot leave this halfway through.
I'll stay until this saga's done,
The victor crowned, the campaign won,
'Till laurel wreath adorns some brow,
And then 'tis time, 'tis time enow
To breathe my last; and in demise
Please gently close my content eyes,

(99)

And bear me to my waiting grave,
To Eppleworth's sweet, quiet enclave:
My spirit swiftly fly away
Past human night and human day
To realms unknown. In fabled vale
I'll meet my friends and tell this tale.
And so astonished they will be
They'll wish they had been there with me.

Maggie's Eye and Jenkin's Ear

This is a song of Maggie's Eye,
Of Maggie's Eye and Jenkin's Ear;
Two dangers faced with hearts held high -
The Ear has gone, the Eye's still here.

Let loud the beat of Drake's old drum
Sound throughout this sceptred isle;
And though the whole wide world should come
In arms; we stand and will not fly.

The Ear, alas, no longer hears,
'Tis but a page of history.
The Eye looks forth both wise and clear,
A lazer shining splendidly.
Two healthy orbs in Maggie's head,
Twin suns shine out in golden health. -
When Jenkin's form was laid to rest
I hope The Ear lay on his breast.

Sad Jenkins lost a treasured Ear,
But Maggie has not lost her Eye;
Dark shadows of a phantom'd fear
Are fled. The day is bright, our hopes are high.

The Young Constable

A first year Constable am I,
Of ruddy cheek and bright clear eye.
My youthful manner, sprightly gait,
Do I repress to ordered pace.
I neither hum, nor skip, nor laugh,
When bent on duty's sober path.
My outward features, well controlled,
Conceal a spirit brave and bold.
I zeal display for all to see,
This Chief Inspector yet to be.

To dolls in blue I show respect,
Especially Inspectors pets;
Give Supers humble deference,
And Magistrates bow'd reverence.
In staff canteen I patient wait
For sausage, mash upon a plate.
Let not my soup spoon careless drip,
Nor ever from a saucer sip.
Attentive, hear how Sergeant brought
The miscreant before the Court.

This, my vocation, I enjoy,
My comrades all do I extol;
Yet when I tread the midnight hour
Through Gorbal's canyons, slow repeat

While danger, boredom, dogs my feet,
The worm of discontent appears
To fill my mind as dawn draws near;
Then do I sadly contemplate
Both pavement and my bank book state.
The tardy, welcome, monthly cheque
But barely keeps me out of debt.
Though it I will not disparage,
'Tis truly not an oil-rig wage.

My Jeanie, temptress, smiles at me,
Oh! that Garden, Serpent, Tree.
She pleads I discard frugal ways,
Embrace a wide-horizon'd day
Of index'd credits, friendly banks
And join, thereby, the modern ranks.
She sweetly speaks beguiling words
Of Visa, Access, Trustee Cards:
Wealth to garner without waiting,
Wealth, like fruit, just for the taking.

Her hands soft touch, her melting glance,
Eternal Eve doth me entrance;
Thus is resistance swept aside,
Deep-drown'd upon a tempests tide.
My forethought wise as scattered spray
On ocean's bosom toss'd away....
Late evening's glow, before my eyes,
Holds promise of a new sunrise:

(103)

Wide vistas of a spacious life
Where doubts are shadows put to flight.

Here in my hand a Banker's Card,
Begone dull care, I you discharge.
I need a car; she clothes, smart shoes,
To keep our life style in the groove.
This magic opens every door
And never need we now be poor.
All problems, worries, cast aside
By thee, thou wonder plastic card.
So, Brave New World, here do I come,
Look out! My spending has but scarce begun.

All times goes on, the years slide by,
The sum of hours they wingéd fly;
New sunsets grace these older skies,
Precursors each of calm sunrise.
And I at ease 'neath wifely glance;
She, strict controller of finance.
My Jeanie, still as fair is she
At roseate maturity.
Youth's waywardness have I abjured,
And wry regard my stolid mores...
I watch new entrant Constables,
Their foolish, transient foibles.
I am a mentor, stern and kind,
Their Chief Inspector, grey and wise.

February

February's silent snows,
So lately come, so slow to go;
Oh how I wish each flake were warm,
The north-east wind a zephyr's balm.

Then would we welcome winter time,
With happy hearts greet season's clime;
The agéd pensioners might sit
On noonday lawns in bronzèd bliss.

All heating systems turned right off,
And deeper snows cure chesty coughs;
Our winter thermals cast astride,
And sorrows go and joys abide.

But halt; 'tis well this cannot be,
For Viking's breed are surely we;
And, hardened by the northern blasts,
Must we confront our frozen paths.

With visage stern and stolid steps
Uphold traditions brave precepts,
And firm withstand the arctic cold
'Midst influenza, ills and woes.

Passivity

The nights pass slow in fragment dreams,
Frail shadows move at open doors,
Pale peering faces of unfinished woes,
Hesitant to enter or to go,
Grey insubstantial ghosts of ghosts,
And I their author and their host.

I early wake to sad and numbered days,
Yet am I happier than I know;
The world of me no notice takes
But, by this indifference does enfold
Within the fabric of life's woven whole
A mild, unchalleng'd, anonymous role.

All men must die and so must I,
And leave behind box'd relic bones;
Meantime my soul to highest Heaven flies,
(For so by thoughtful bishops am I told);
But, of bones and souls, what e're they state,
there is no choice; I wait for Heaven's grace.

The Young Ballerina

A limping Maid left London grim,
Her Toe a crooked, painful thing,
She travell'd north to pleasant parts
To rustic folk with pensive hearts.
And while the Toe received repair,
The Maiden breath'd a purer air.

In gentle verdant Anlaby
That Toe was pulled so skillfully
It fits in now, in happy mood,
The frictionless, appointed groove.
Thus Foot below has naught to fear,
And Face above portrays no care.

As she flies through the air with the greatest if ease,
Our charming young Nymph cannot fail to please,
For her 'leaps' are exquisite; her 'pirouettes' quite divine,
Her instructor enraptur'd by a skill so sublime.
So a toast to the Toe, and a cheer for the Puller,
The one's in great shape because of the other.

Ode to Christine

Oh fair and friendly lady
Whose golden gaze
Doth frequent fall upon
The Chelsea Green
Where high and silver clouds
Do silent sail
Across an azure sea,
Where dawn and dusk
In ordered style
'Twixt sunlit day
And moon lit night
Perform their scheduled tasks
Upon thy nearby fields.

Oh handsome, peerless lady
As a rose thou goes about thy ways
Thy kindly nature, pleasant air,
Doth fully mirror and reflect
The gracious heart within,
A mirror true portrayed
Upon thy face.
And high above her head
The silvered clouds sail on
To their cherished island seas,
And fair Christine herself
Enmeshed within an enclosed world

Should journey soft with them,
In mind's hope and trust
To a waiting amethyst isle,
Where waving palms
Gently move Pacific airs,
And where thou, Christine,
Upon a coral shore,
In your own heart's ease,
may sweetly dream
Thy cares away.